Copyright

Copyright © 2020 by Erica Basora
All rights reserved. This book or any portion thereof may not be reproduced or used in any manner whatsoever without the express written permission of the publisher except for the use of brief quotations in a book review.

Publisher: That's Love Publishing LLC
Printed in the United States of America

ISBN 978-1-953751-00-3

Orders by U.S. trade bookstores
and wholesalers.
Please contact E. Basora
at thatslovepublishing@gmail.com
Website: thatslovepublishing.com

Dedication

To the Proverbs 31 Women in my life who inspired this book. To my beautiful Mom, who has always demonstrated joy even during the storm and for being an example of the love of Christ. To my MomE, who exemplified a woman after God's own heart. Thank you for always encouraging me to be who God has created me to be, to walk in my calling, and to practice my gift especially my writing.
Miss you with all my heart.

My Mom is a great example of the Proverbs 31 woman. I think your Mommy, Nana, Granny, Auntie, or Mother figure may be the Proverbs 31 woman model in your life. This story is for me and for all of you.

My Mommy is the best of her kind.
She is more valuable than any jewels
you can find.

"A wife of noble character who can find? She is worth far more than rubies." Proverbs 31:10

She does a wonderful job juggling our world.
We never end up in a whirl.

"Her husband has full confidence in her and lacks nothing of value." Proverbs 31:11

Mommy keeps us safe from harm.
She teaches us to do the right thing, even when someone is twisting our arm.

"She brings him good, not harm,
all the days of her life." Proverbs 31:12

She is eager to try new things, especially with me. Mommy says, "Always remember, the best gift is one made with love which is always free."

"She selects wool and flax and works with eager hands." Proverbs 31:13

We drive all over town on shopping days. Mommy likes to buy things and uses coupons when she pays.

"She is like the merchant ships, bringing her food from afar." Proverbs 31:14

Before the sun says hello, Mommy is awake, getting us ready for the day. Some days I get my favorite breakfast; French toast, with cream cheese and maple syrup, served on a tray.

"She gets up while it is still night; she provides food for her family and portions for her servant girls." Proverbs 31:15

Mommy dreamed of one day owning her own space, and today we live in her dream place. She planted a garden full of her favorite flowers. I sometimes play in it and pretend I have secret powers.

"She considers a field and buys it; out of her earnings she plants a vineyard." Proverbs 31:16

Mommy is strong and works without ceasing. She does a variety of things like weeding her garden, helping me with school projects and making sure our laundry pile is not increasing.

"She sets about her work vigorously; her arms are strong for her tasks." Proverbs 31:17

Mommy learns to use new tools and technology. To help my siblings and I with our homework, like Biology.

"In her hand she holds the distaff and grasps the spindle with her fingers." Proverbs 31:19

Mommy teaches us to love our neighbors and to give freely. She shows us how to love the poor and those who are needy. She donates items and volunteers. She encourages me to help my peers.

"She opens her arms to the poor and extends her hands to the needy." Proverbs 31:20

When winter comes, Mommy bundles us up tight.
She lives without fear and has raised us to
be bright.

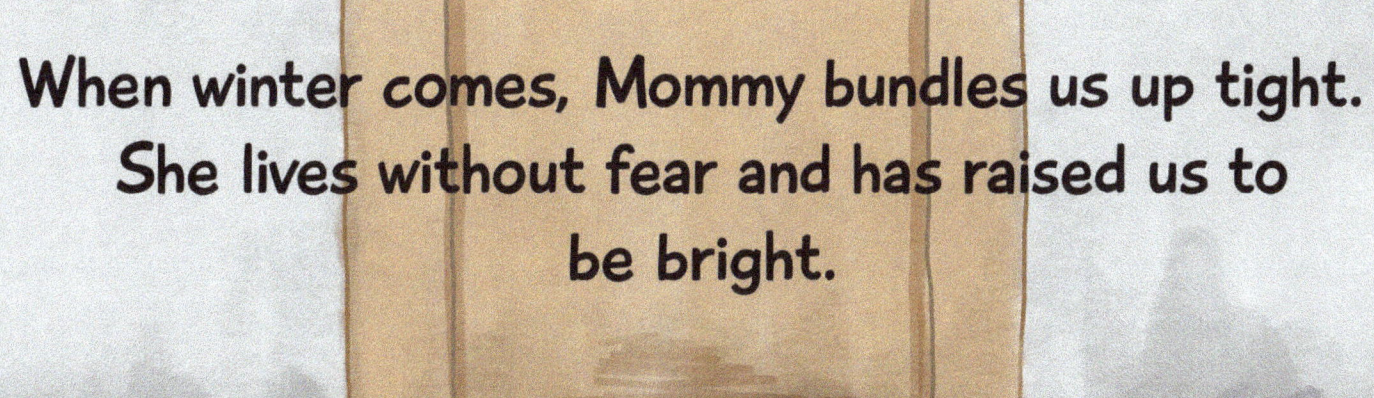

"When it snows, she has no fear for her household for all of them are clothed in scarlet." Proverbs 31: 21

Mommy loves fashion, especially her costume jewelry and accessories. Her dresses are beautiful and looks like royalty, not just on her anniversaries.

"She makes coverings for her bed she is clothed in fine linen and purple." Proverbs 31: 22

What I love best about my mommy is that she is full of wisdom. Mommy teaches us about God's kingdom.

"She speaks with wisdom and faithful instruction is on her tongue." Proverbs 31:26

Mommy keeps our house in order.
She makes sure she spends time with me as I get older.

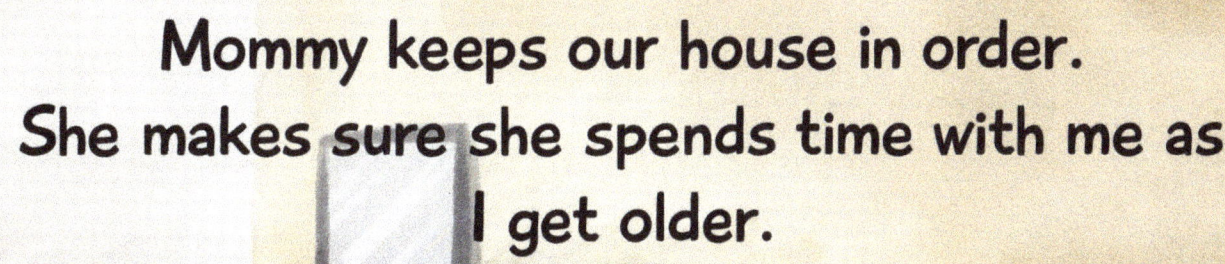

"She watches over the affairs of her household and does not eat the bread of idleness." Proverbs 31:27

I am grateful to have my mommy and will always confess, we rise up, and call her Blessed.

"Her children arise and call her blessed her husband also, and he praises her." Proverbs 31:28

You may have a Mommy, Nana, Granny, Auntie, or mother figure, "She is blessed," is what you will call. For me, my mommy is the best of them all.

"Many women do noble things, but you surpass them all." Proverbs 31:29

Even though my mommy is getting older and her hair is changing color. I see her love for the Lord growing stronger.

"Charm is deceptive, and beauty is fleeting but a woman who fears the LORD is to be praised." Proverbs 31:30

My mom deserves a great reward.
Which God has stored. One day, she will be given
a beautiful crown, to go along with
a beautiful gown.

"Honor her for all that her hands have done, and let her works bring her praise at the city gate." Proverbs 31:31

God loves you and one day you may be a Mommy. May you understand who God wants you to be for your family. Today we pray that you have a woman like the Mommy described in this story in your life. May you celebrate her, feel her love for you, and understand that you are part of God's love story.

www.ingramcontent.com/pod-product-compliance
Lightning Source LLC
Chambersburg PA
CBHW041234240426
43673CB00010B/334